DINOSAUR ESCAPE MAZES

by Roger Moreau

Sterling Publishing Co., Inc.
New York

15 14 13 12 11 10 9 8 7

Published by Sterling Publishing Co., Inc.

387 Park Avenue South, New York, N.Y. 10016

© 2002 by Roger Moreau

Distributed in Canada by Sterling Publishing

C/o Canadian Manda Group, 165 Dufferin Street

Toronto, Ontario, Canada M6K 3H6

Distributed in the United Kingdom by GMC Distribution Services

Castle Place, 166 High Street, Lewes, East Sussex, England BN7 1XU

Distributed in Australia by Capricorn Link (Australia) Pty. Ltd.

P.O. Box 704, Windsor, NSW 2756 Australia

Printed in China

Sterling ISBN 0-8069-5519-8

For information about custom editions, special sales, premium and

corporate purchases, please contact Sterling Special Sales

Department at 800-805-5489 or specialsales@sterlingpub.com

Contents

A Note on the Suggested Use of this Book

As you work your way through the pages of this book, try not to mark them. This will enable you to take this journey over and over again and will give your friends a chance to take the same journey that you took with all of the same dangers that you had to face.

Special Warning: When the way looks too difficult, avoid the temptation to start at the end and work your way backwards. This technique would be a violation of the rules and could result in your getting eaten by a dinosaur.

Cover maze: This *Tyrannosaurus rex* has decided to block your path and eat you for lunch. Escape by running under him to the safety of the forest. Find a clear path.

Introduction

On August 19, 1909, in the Uinta Basin of eastern Utah, scientist Earl Douglass came upon eight tailbones of a fossilized dinosaur. Douglass had been hired to find specimens for the new Carnegie Museum of Natural History in Pittsburgh, Pennsylvania.

Douglass could be considered one of the first paleontologists. A paleontologist is a scientist trained in the study of fossils. Paleontologists extract fossils from the ground, study them, and attempt to reassemble them into the creature they once were.

Over the years, a vast number of fossils has been unearthed in this basin where Douglass had his success. It is now known as Dinosaur National Monument.

Our story begins here. Several years later, another scientist came to the area with a young apprentice. This apprentice was so excited by the work that he went on to study at an eastern university, where he obtained his doctorate in paleontology (fossil science). He has since become one of the most respected and renowned paleontologists in the world. His name is Dr. Theodore Rex.

Dr. Rex founded the Museum of Natural History in Dinosaur City, Utah, where he has assembled one of the largest collection of dinosaur fossils in the world. Now 89 years old and in failing health, Dr. Rex is considering retirement. There is no question that scientists throughout the world recognize the accomplishments the doctor has made in the field of dinosaur study.

But this is not all that Dr. Rex has accomplished. There is one final thing that he must do before retirement. Secretly, in the back rooms of the museum, the doctor has been involved in what he feels will be the greatest contribution of all to the study of dinosaurs—his time machine. In his early years of study, Dr. Rex discovered a vortex that allows people to travel back in time. He realized that a high-speed flying disc could pass through the vortex and return to a time in the past. He has worked continuously on this time machine for the past 60 years, and now thinks that it is complete and ready to be tested. He would make the test himself, but his age and frailty will not allow it. He must find someone who would be willing to face the many dangers of such a test. Would it work? How much fuel would it take? Could it return? And, also, what would be the dangers there? These are all unanswered questions.

It was just the other day, while the doctor was sharing his secret concerns with a close friend, that your name came up. The doctor immediately wrote you a letter, which you must read. It is on the following page.

Below is the letter written to you by Dr. Theodore Rex:

Museum of Natural History
4128 Jurassic Avenue
Dinosaur City, Utah 89721

Dear friend:

A friend of mine who thinks very highly of you gave me your name, and so I am writing this letter to you.

My name is Dr. Theodore Rex and I am a paleontologist at the museum. Simply, I study dinosaur bones. As a spokesperson on behalf of the scientific world regarding these studies, I am asking you for your help. Please read what I have written below and then carefully consider your decision, which I hope will be to accept my request.

In the early years of my studies, I discovered that it is possible to go back in time through a complex time vortex. Without going into the details as to how this works, suffice it to say I have created a machine that, I hope, will enable a person to journey to a specific time in history. Of course, the time frame I have chosen to program into the machine is the Jurassic Period, that of the dinosaurs. The person I would like to make that journey is you.

It would be unfair not to inform you of some of the unknowns regarding the time machine. You must know that it has not been tested. I am not sure how much fuel will be required to transport someone to the Jurassic Period. It does operate on natural gases so, should you accept this mission, you would have to take a gas container in case you run out of gas and need to find some there. In that period there should be plenty of gas bogs around. I have confidence that if the machine can get you there, it will be able to get you home.

Finally, there will undoubtedly be great hazards there. At all cost, avoid raptors and *Tyrannosaurus rex*—especially nesting ones, as I have discovered that a mother *T. rex* when nesting is even more ferocious than a male!

I know this is asking a lot, but you will be making a priceless contribution to science. If all goes well and the time machine works, think of all the possibilities.

Should you decide to take the trip, come to my office in the museum, where you will find the machine. I will be unable to be there, but I will have everything ready for your departure. Just enter the time machine, turn all switches to "on" in numerical order, and work the guidance controls to the Jurassic Period on the monitor. Good luck.

Thank you for your kind consideration of this very important project.

Sincerely,

Dr. Theodore Rex

The Natural History Museum

Find your way to the museum by advancing on a green light. Go straight, and turn left or right on green.

The Laboratory

Find your way to Dr. Rex's office by making your way around the doctor's work.

Enter

Dr. Rex's Office

The office is a mess, but do not disturb anything. Find a clear passage to the time machine.

The Flight Control Panel

With all engines on, control the guidance system to the time zone "Jurassic Period" by working your way through the grid openings. If you take too long, you could run out of fuel.

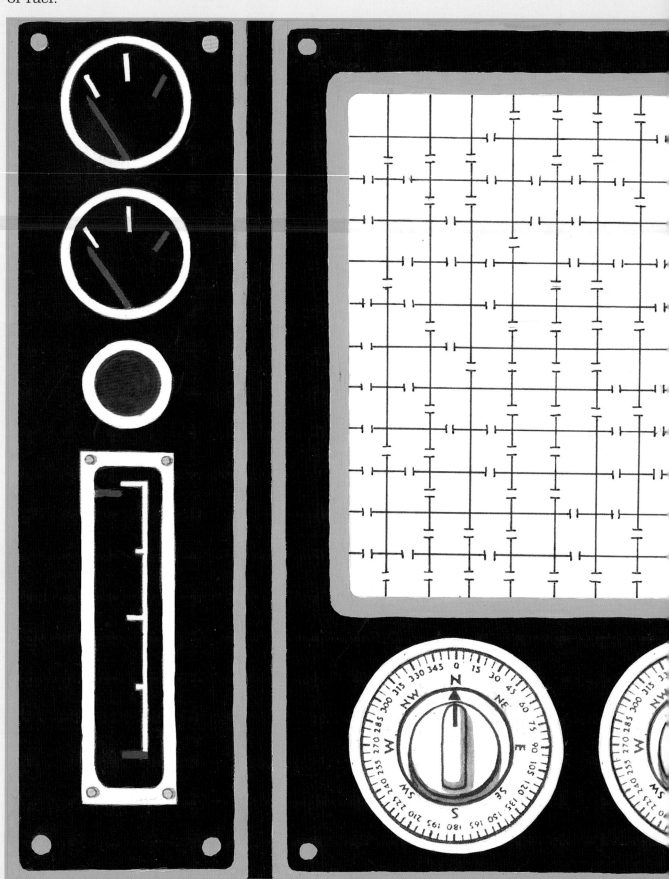

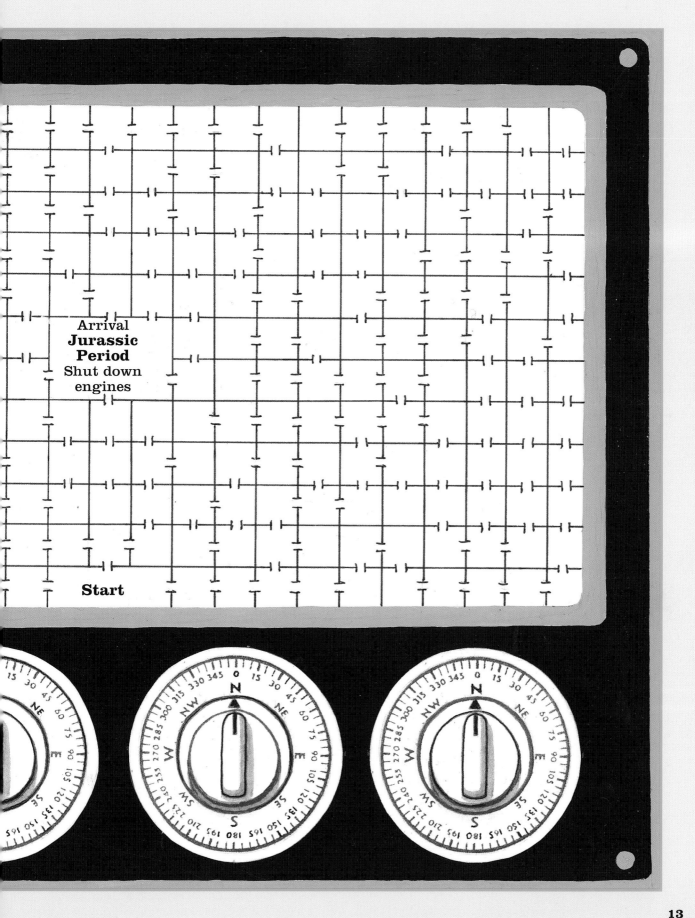

Arrival
Jurassic Period
Shut down engines

Start

Shut Down *Now!*

You're out of fuel. Shut down the system in numerical order or damage could result.

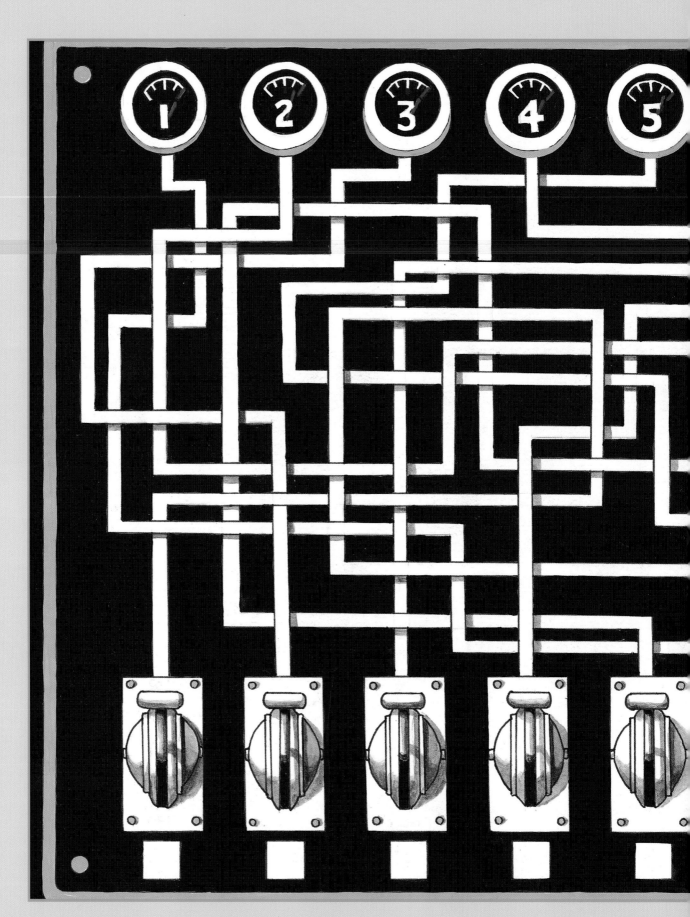

The *T. Rex* Nest

You couldn't have landed in a worse spot—a *Tyrannosaurus rex* nest. Escape in a hurry by finding a clear path before Mother arrives.

Here Comes Mother

Don't stop...keep moving. Find a clear path.

Oh No! Mom and Dad!

No time to rest. Head for the safety of that cave. Find a clear path.

Start
Head for
the cave

The Cave

At last, a chance to rest! You'd better set out to find a source of fuel for the time machine so you can get home. A gas pond will work…maybe. Find your way through the cave without disturbing the occupants.

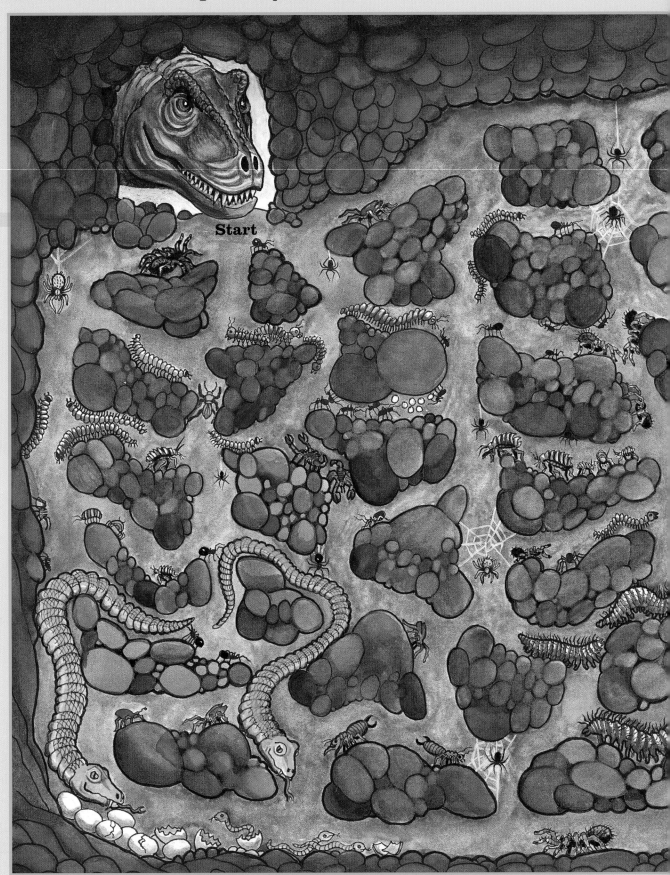

Start

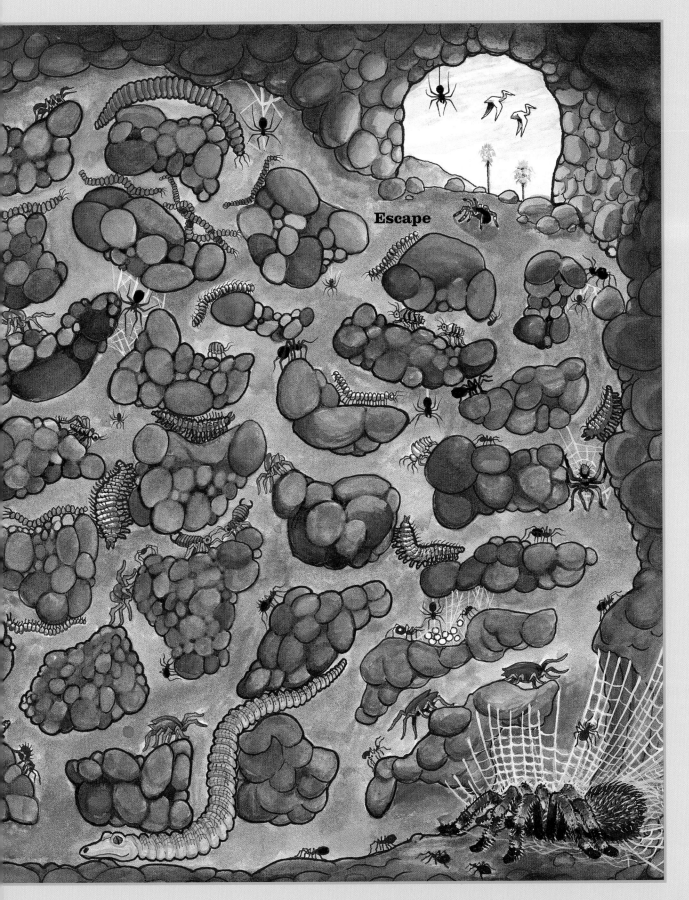

Escape

Raptors!

You'd better hurry down the hill. Avoid the rocks.

Start

Escape

A *Stegosaurus* Herd

There's danger here. Carefully work your way around the dinosaurs and head for the river.

The River

Continue your search for fuel. Cross the river on the connecting rocks.

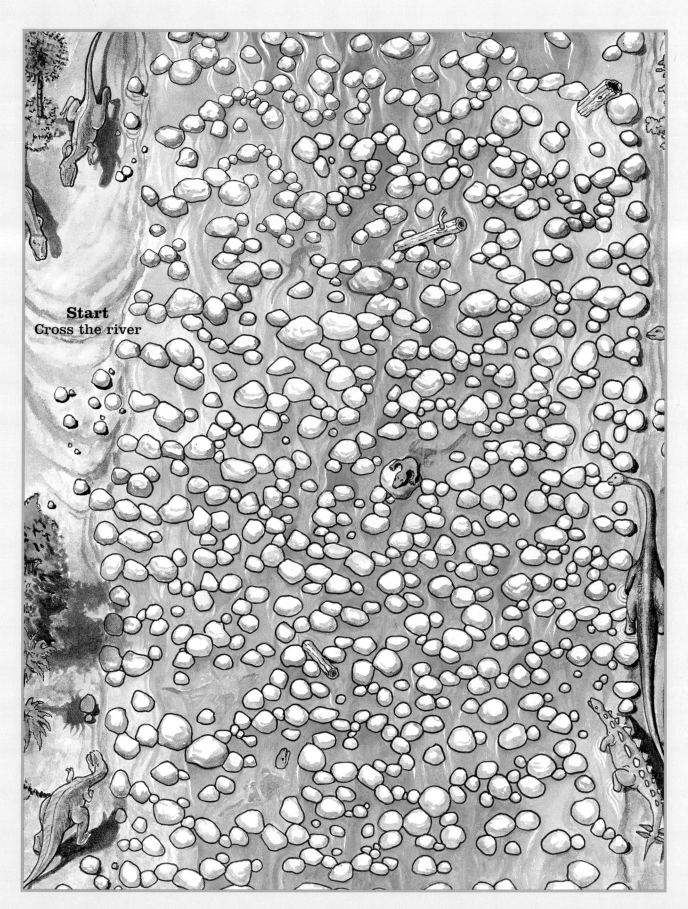

Start
Cross the river

The Valley

Search through the valley until you get to the other side. Dinosaurs lurk everywhere, so be careful. Find a clear path.

Start on this side

Exit on
this side

The Mountains

Find a clear path through the canyons to reach the other side of this mountain range.

Start on this side

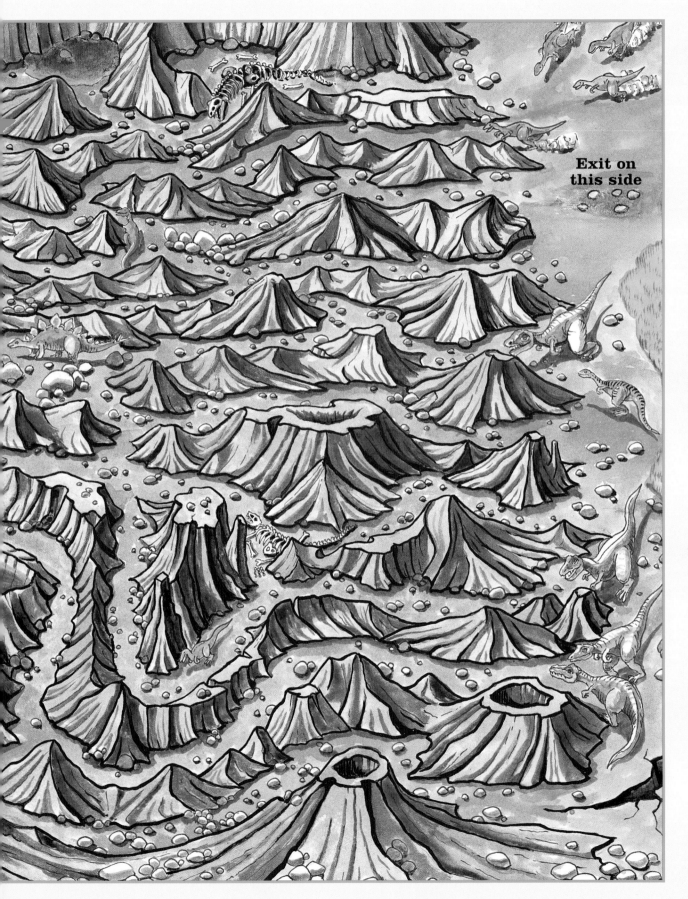

Exit on
this side

The Lake

This will be dangerous. Swim across the lake and avoid the creatures under and above the water. Find a clear course to swim.

Start

Exit

Canyons

You'd better hurry here. Those raptors are not friendly. Find your way across the canyons by crossing the logs. Hide in the forest.

Hide in the forest

Start

The Forest

More raptors! Climb the vines to reach the top vine. Once you start on a vine you cannot cross onto another vine until you reach the top.

She's Back!

Mother *T. rex* is not giving up. Descend the vines fast. Be sure to pick the right one.

The Roots

Cross the right root to the other side of the canyon. Do not cross from one root to the other.

Two *Pachycephalosauri*

These two are looking for someone to pound. You're it! Hurry to the safety on the canyon edge. Find a clear path.

Start

Safety
here

Nesting *Pteranodons*

This doesn't look good. Descend on the connecting rocks and avoid the nesting *Pteranodons*. It looks like a chance to rest at the bottom.

Rest here

Stampeding *Triceratops*

Your rest is over. You've got just minutes to get to the other side of the canyon and climb the connecting rocks to the safety of the ledge. Avoid the cracks.

Start

The Gas Bog

Gas is bubbling up in the middle of this bog. Cross over on the dinosaur bones to the gas, fill your container (you did bring a container, didn't you?), and begin your return to the time machine.

Eruption!

That volcano has finally let go. Hurry past all of the stampeding dinosaurs. Find a clear path.

Exit on this side

Start on
this side

Flaming Rocks

Keep on the move. The flaming rocks and lava flow are getting worse. Find a clear path.

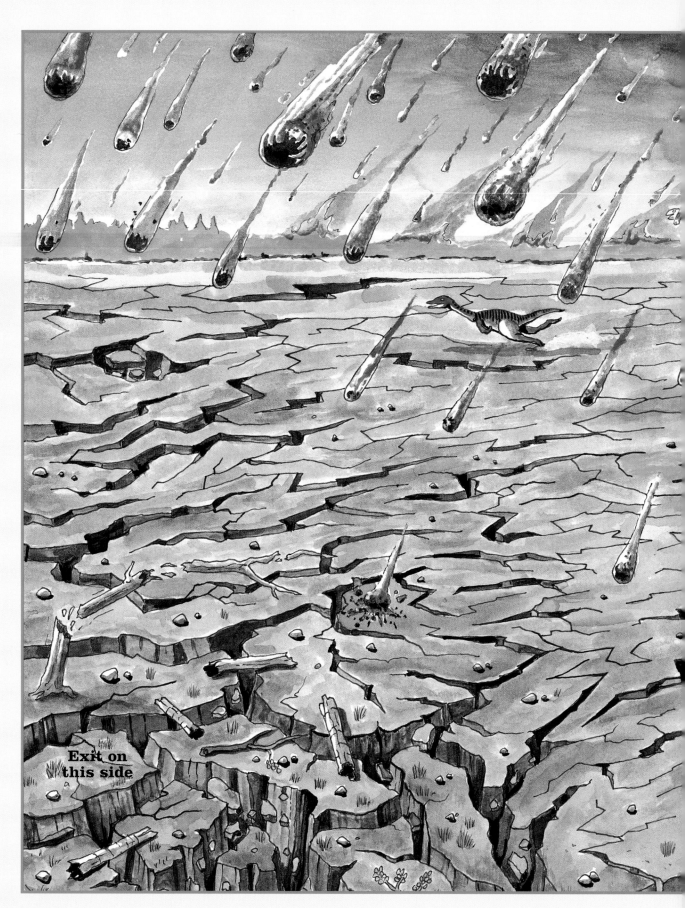

Start on
this side

The Time Machine

You must get to the time machine before the lava does. Good luck!

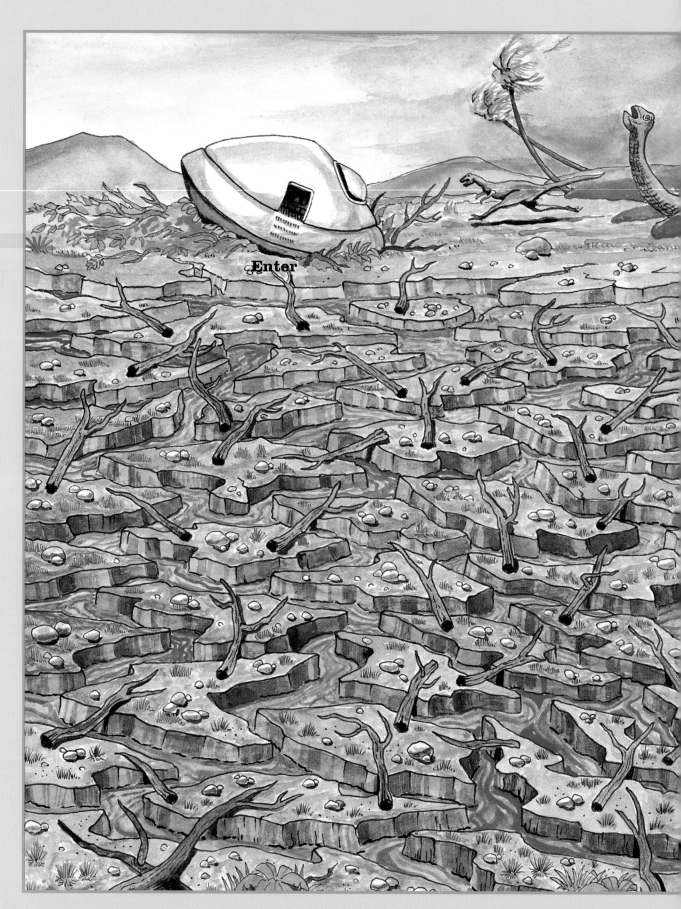

Enter

Start

Fire Up the Engines!

With the fuel tanks full, push all levers to the "on" position in numerical order. Hurry!

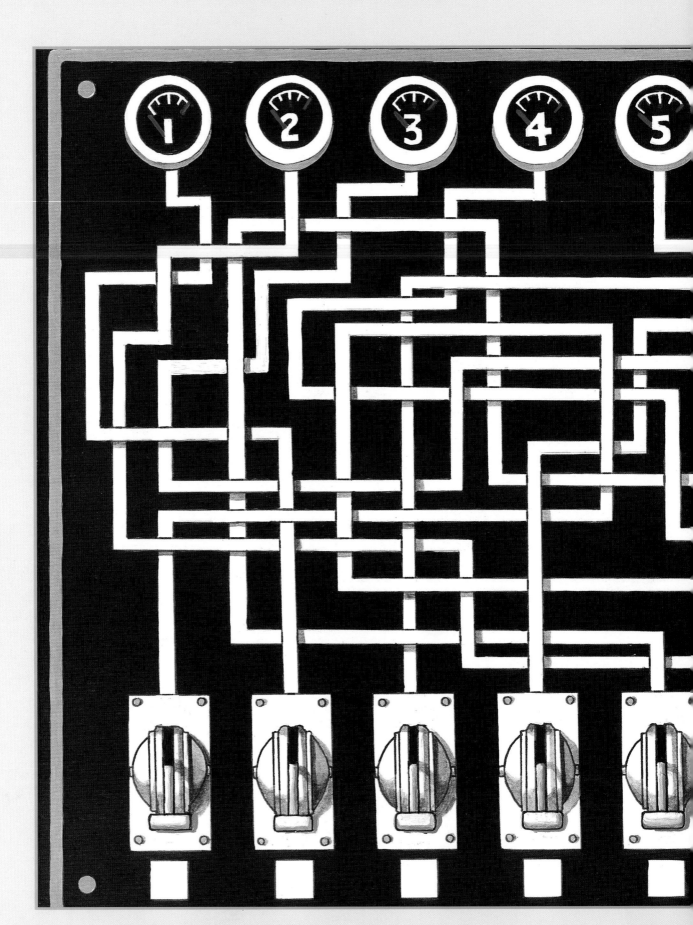

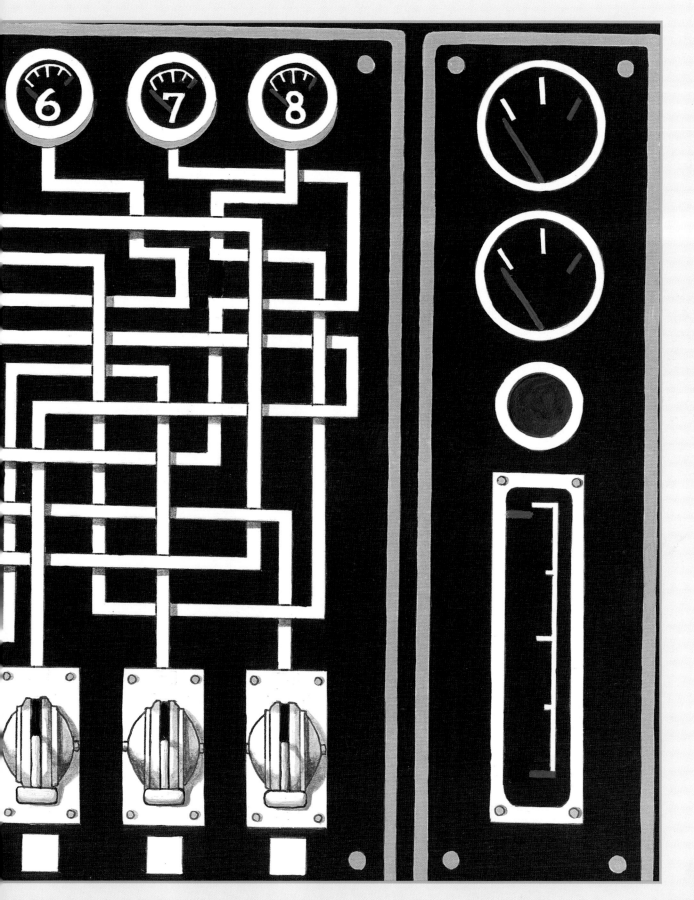

Congratulations

Somehow you managed to survive this ordeal. Doctor Theodore Rex will be thrilled to know his time machine worked, even though there are a few bugs to work out. More important, however, than all of the wonderful potential that the time machine has and the experience of going back in time, is the discovery that you've made regarding the type of person you are. You can feel confident that you'll be able to handle the most difficult situations in the future with courage, determination, strength, and grit. This experience has proven that. Most people would have given up if put into the same circumstances that you recently faced. But you didn't, because you're not a quitter.

Solutions to all of the mazes are on the following pages.

Cover Solution/The Natural History Museum

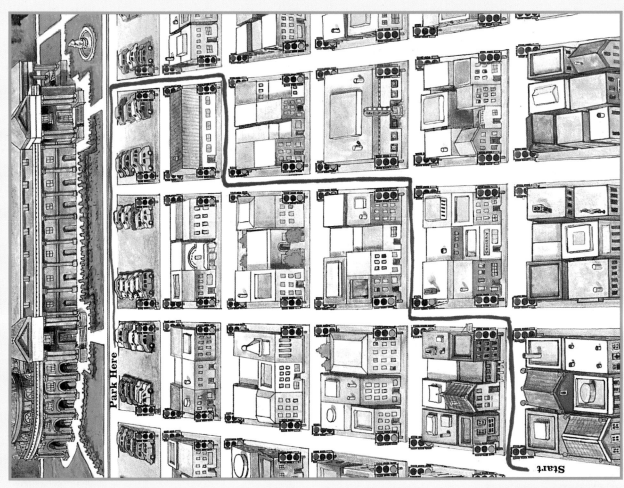

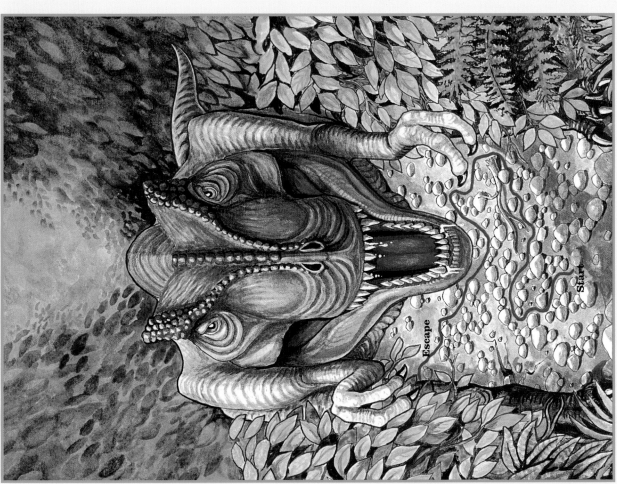

The Laboratory

Arrival
Jurassic
Period
Shut down
engines

Start

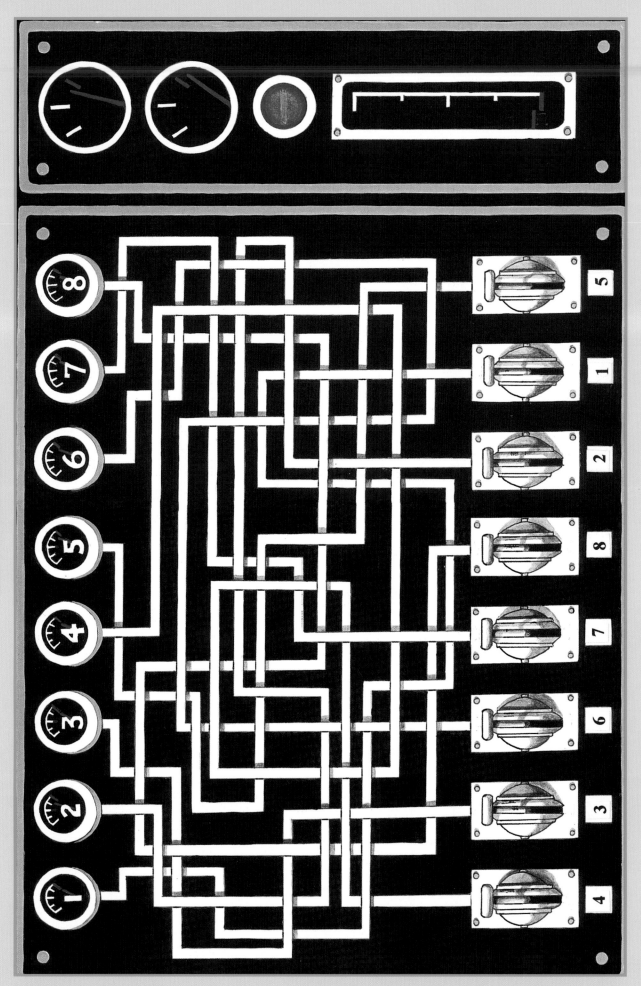

Shut Down Now!

57

The *T. Rex* Nest

Start

Escape

Here Comes Mother

Start

Escape

Start
Head for
the cave

The Cave

Escape

Start

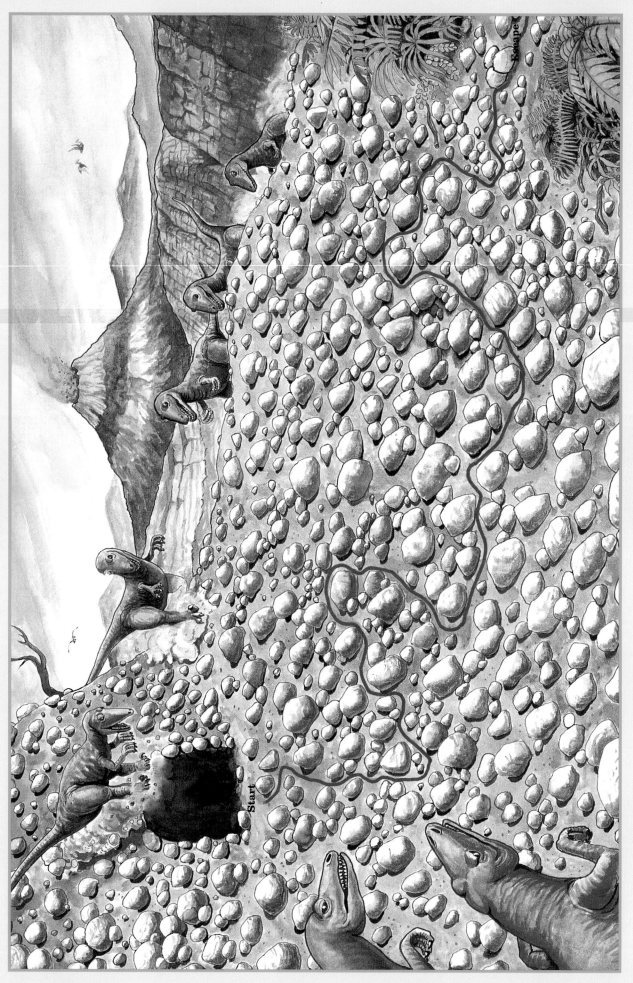

Raptors!

A *Stegosaurus* Herd

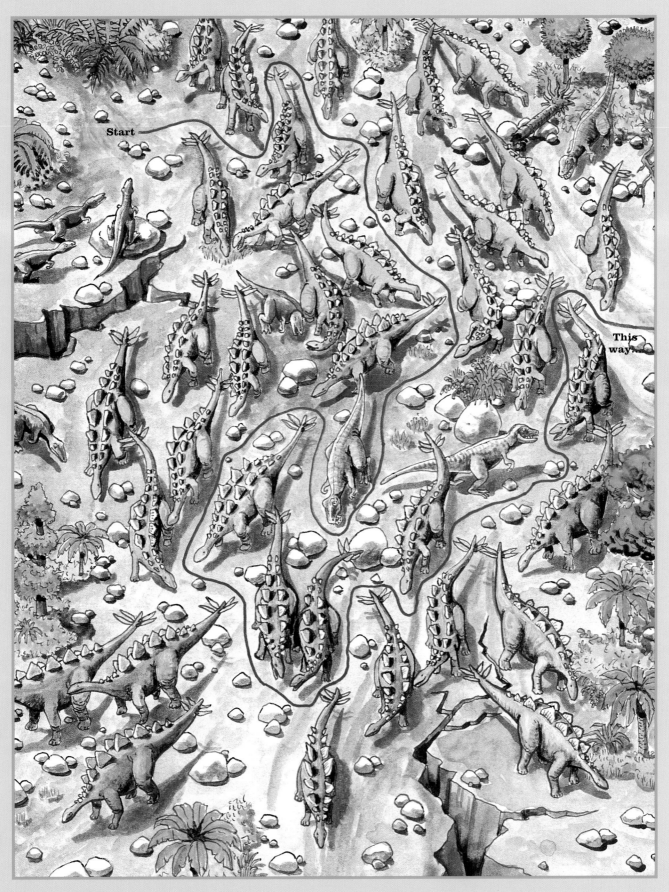

Start

This way!

The River

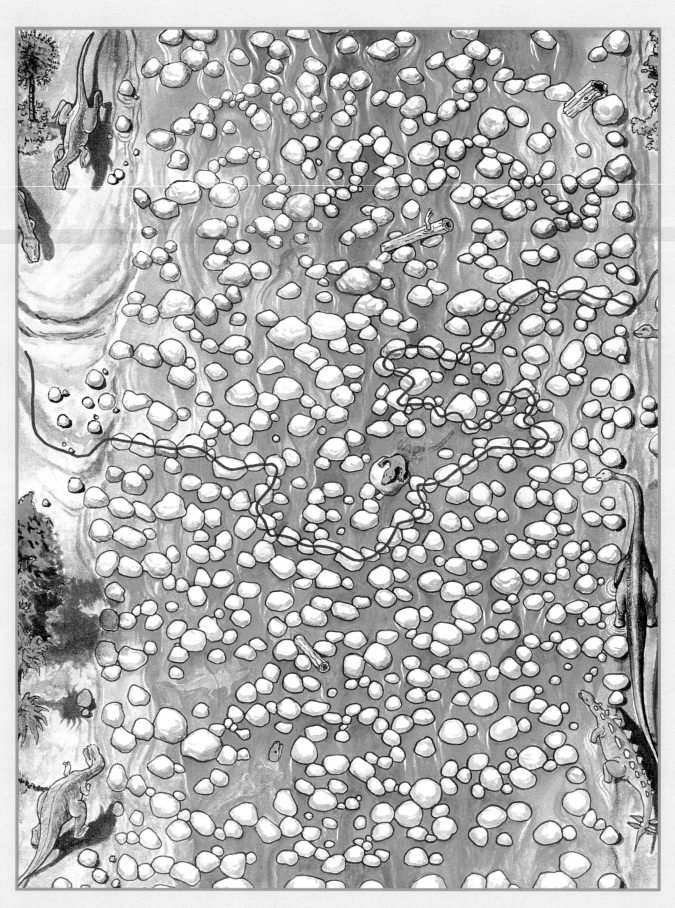

The Valley

Exit on this side

Start on this side

The Mountains

Start on this side

Exit on this side

The Lake

Exit

Start

Canyons

Hide in the forest

Start

The Forest

She's Back!

The Roots

Start

This way...

Two Pachycephalosauri

Nesting *Pteranodons*

Start

Rest
here

73

Stampeding Triceratops

Safety here

Start

The Gas Bog

Return to ship

Start

Eruption!

Start on this side

Exit on this side

Flaming Rocks

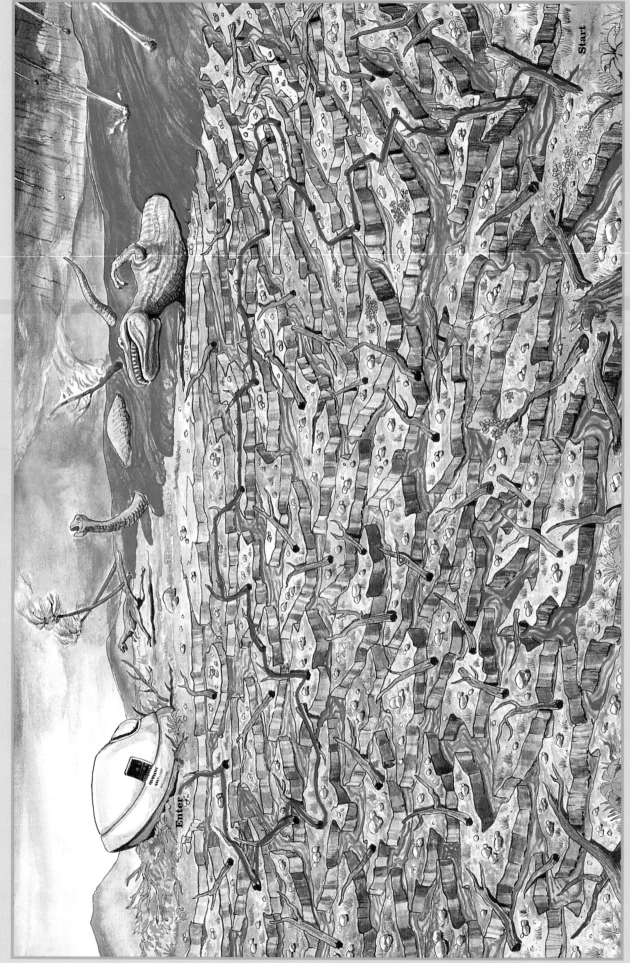

The Time Machine

Fire Up the Engines!

Index

Page numbers in **bold** refer to answer mazes.